The Law of Attraction & Manifestation Mastery

Understand the Advanced Techniques to Manifest an Abundance of Love, Success, Money, Health and Happiness, so you can be Empowered to Take Control of Your Destiny

Olivia Clifford

"The Law of Attraction & Manifestation Mastery: Understand the Advanced Techniques to Manifest an Abundance of Love, Success, Money, Health and Happiness, so you can be Empowered to Take Control of Your Destiny". Written By "Olivia Clifford".

The Law of Attraction & Manifestation Mastery is a bundle of the books "Law of Attraction—Beginners Guide" & "Manifesting – Beginners Guide".

Hope You Enjoy!

© **Copyright 2021 – All rights reserved.**

The content contained within this book may not be reproduced, duplicated or transmitted without direct written permission from the author or the publisher.

Under no circumstances will any blame or legal responsibility be held against the publisher, or author, for any damages, reparation, or monetary loss due to the information contained within this book, either directly or indirectly.

Legal Notice:

This book is copyright protected. It is only for personal use. You cannot amend, distribute, sell, use, quote or paraphrase any part, or the content within this book, without the consent of the author or publisher.

Disclaimer Notice:

Please note the information contained within this document is for educational and entertainment purposes only. All effort has been executed to present accurate, up to date, reliable, complete information. No warranties of any kind are declared or implied. Readers acknowledge that the author is not engaged in the rendering of legal, financial, medical or professional advice. The content within this book has been derived from various sources. Please consult a licensed professional before attempting any techniques outlined in this book.

By reading this document, the reader agrees that under no circumstances is the author responsible for any losses, direct or indirect, that are incurred as a result of the use of the information contained within this document, including, but not limited to, errors, omissions, or inaccuracies.

Table of Contents

Law of Attraction—Beginners Guide

Introduction

Chapter 1: Shift Your Energy

Chapter 2: Manifestation

Chapter 3: Love Thyself

Chapter 4: Abundance is All Around You

Chapter 5: Healthy Mind, Healthy Body, Healthy Life

Chapter 6: Attracting Your Dream Life

Conclusion

References

Manifesting – Beginners Guide

Introduction

Chapter 1: The Law of Attraction

Chapter 2: The Power of Now

Chapter 3: Moving Into Alignment and Staying There

Chapter 4: Get Out of Your Own Way - Overcome Self-Sabotage

Chapter 5: The Secret Behind Manifesting

Chapter 6: Live Life Fully

Final Thoughts

References

Law of Attraction—Beginners Guide

Proven Principles and Techniques to Make the Law of Attraction Work for Relationships, Money, Weight Loss, Love, and Business So You Can Live Your Dream Life

Olivia Clifford

Introduction

If you can think of it, you can create it. This is the premise of the Law of Attraction—that whatever it is that we desire we simply request of the Universe and we will receive it. If this is true, then why aren't we all living out our wildest dreams? Why are we still asking and not receiving? Why does it seem as if the Law of Attraction works for the rich and famous, but not for people like you or me?

You are here because you want to learn how to tap into this unseen power that will magically transform your life. You want the fastest road to success and you want it yesterday. What you must first understand is that the Law of Attraction is, and has been, working to bring you what you ask for. "Then why am I not rich?" "Why have I not met the person of my dreams?" "Why do I not have the car, house, or job I've been asking for?"

The problem is not that you haven't been asking for what you want, it's that you are still focused on what you don't want or have. What most people misunderstand about the Law of Attraction is that there is much more to attracting what you desire than just asking. This is why it has failed to bring you what you say you desire.

You did not come here by chance, even in deciding to read this book the Law of Attraction is working for you. The universe is providing you an opportunity to change your life in the way you want. In the pages of this book, you will not learn how to get everything you dream of. You will learn how to attract the people, experiences, and things that will lead you to live the life of your dreams. You will learn the secrets of using the Law of Attraction to manifest your deepest desires.

Once you understand how the Law of Attraction works, you will begin to live with more intention. You will stop reacting and start responding to life. How you respond is what will flow back to you. It's a very simple concept that takes conscious awareness. That is what you are about to gain.

Chapter 1: Shift Your Energy

The Law of Attraction is always in motion. Every thought, emotion, and response you experience fuels what flows to you because of the Law of Attraction. This law states that what you focus on is what you receive. You are the constant creator of your own reality. This is no foreign concept. Celebrities, entrepreneurs, and some of the most successful people around the world credit all that they have accomplished to the Law of Attraction. Does that mean this law favors the wealthy and famous? No.

Millions of people have transformed their lives by understanding and embracing the Law of Attraction. They may not have reached fame and incredible fortune, but they have created a life that is filled with love, happiness, health, and abundance. They are living the life of their dreams and are continuously attracting more of what they want. In this chapter, you will begin to understand how the Law of Attraction is working for you.

Ancient Techniques

Though the Law of Attraction became widely known when *The Secret* was released, it is a practice that has been around for centuries. The practices, principles, and concepts that make up the Law of Attraction have been written in many religious texts and hinted at throughout history.

Buddha has been quoted saying, "All that we are is a result of what we have thought" (Hurst, n.d.). Jesus hints at limitless power to create, suggesting that the Law of Attraction, whether consciously or not, has been a part of our history since the earliest days (Hurst, n.d.).

Meditation, Qigong, manifestation are all ancient practices that have a connection to what we now call the Law of Attraction. Meditation is a practice favored to balance the chakras, or energy centers of the body, and bridge the connection between mind and spirit. Qigong translates to energy work and has been practiced for thousands of years. Manifestation was a practice of the Greek gods that later became a process of aligning the inner self with a higher being.

After the 19th century and before *The Secret* debuted, the Law of Attraction started to garner more attention. Many individuals began to share their own ideas and teachings that took inspiration from ancient techniques.

- Helena Blavatsky was known for her spiritual gifts in the 19th century and wrote *The Secret Doctrine*. The book is a compilation of her thoughts and teachings, much of which relates to the Law of Attraction.
- William Walker Atkinson wrote over 100 books and was co-editor of the *New Thought Journal*. He focused on teaching manifestation.
- Napoleon Hill who wrote *Think and Grow Rich*, one of the most popular self-development books of the past 100 years, shares several highly effective manifestation tools.
- Jerry and Ester Hicks were well-known in the 1980s for spreading the explanation of the Law of attraction. Ester Hicks is also the author of *The Teaching of Abraham, a* popular series that shares his wisdom of the Law of Attraction and manifestation techniques.
- Louise Hay made positive affirmations popular and focused on sharing how others should use self-love and self-compassion to benefit from the Law of Attraction.

Each of these individuals began to bring to light the Law of Attraction (Hurst, n.d.). But these teachings, as beneficial as they are, only tell part of the story. There is also a scientific side to working the Law of Attraction that must be understood.

Quantum Physics/Mechanics

Everything is made of energy. Even our thoughts are composed of millions of energy particles. The Law of Attraction is deeply rooted in this concept. Everything in life is connected through millions of tiny atoms of energy. This energy, which is found in all things, generates frequencies that ebb and flow from one source to another.

Our thoughts are shown to release different frequencies. The energy that we release also attracts energy of the same frequency. We can create a life of abundance, love, and happiness when we keep ourselves aligned to the high-frequency energies flowing around us. This is done when we intentionally give off these higher frequencies.

Core Principle

Like attracts like, but so does dislike. When many believe that the Law of Attraction isn't working for them, they neglect to accept that while they are expecting to receive what they desire, the Law of Attraction does not just work to give back the good in our life. The Law of Attraction is always working because energy is always flowing around us. If we do not consciously become aware of what energy we are giving out to the Universe, we will continue to attract that which we find undesirable.

The more positivity we feed our mind the more we will manifest positive things in our life. The more positive actions we perform, the more of the same we get in return.

Gratitude

Many Law of Attraction techniques include some form of gratitude practice. Science has shown that individuals who express gratitude benefit from lower stress and anxiety, as well as fewer mental and physical health issues (Brown and Wong, 2017). With the Law of Attraction, gratitude is a tool that not only expresses your desires but raises your vibration. Gratitude is a simple practice that many take for granted. You may express thanks when something good happens, but when times get tough we often fail to see what we already have.

Making gratitude a daily practice impacts your thinking, which influences what you attract. Before you go to bed don't just think about all the good that happens during your day; dig deeper and give thanks for all that you can do. Your body and mind have accomplished so much and we tend to ignore all that we are capable of because of our minds and bodies. Think of all the actions you performed during that day that are only possible because of how your magnificent brain is able to sort and store information. Think about all the strength, muscles, and nerves that go into being able to walk, brush your teeth, or open a door. Without our body's ability to move and work together as a cohesive unit, many of the things we do would not be possible.

When we begin to look more closely at all the things that are made possible because of what we have, what we can do, and what we have experienced, greater things start to happen. This is why gratitude is a crucial component of the Law of Attraction. If we do not recognize all that have we will not attract more.

Get into the habit of making gratitude a part of your daily routine. Start by just recognizing three good things that occurred through your day, three people that you are thankful for in your life, or just three things that made you smile. Then, expand on this. Identify the experiences that you are grateful for because of the lesson they have taught you. Highlight the skills that you are capable of. Find meaning and value in the things you do naturally that you don't acknowledge enough. Be grateful for waking in the morning and taking another breath. Be thankful for the roof over your head, the job you have that allows you to support yourself and/or your family (even if you are not particularly fond of your job). The more gratitude you express, the more abundant your life will become.

Chapter 2: Manifestation

There is no limit to what you can have in life. Whatever you can bring to life in your mind you can bring to life in reality. Manifestation is a key practice for those who want to benefit from the Law of Attraction. Manifestation is a misunderstood practice that many believe is just thinking happy thoughts. As you will learn in this chapter, there is more that goes into manifestation than just wishful thinking.

Unlock The Power Of Manifestation

Manifesting involves the conscious, subconscious, and superconscious mind. It is not just about creating a vision of what you desire; it is about fully experiencing this vision as your reality. When we imagine the life we wish to be living, we can alter our perception of the world around us. This change in perception is what will allow you to attract what you desire in life.

Key conditions to manifesting:

- **Desire or Fear**—Many of the things we attract in life are attracted out of fear. We fear not being able to afford things, we fear not finding the right partner, we fear not working a successful job. Fear can be beneficial, but it more often interferes with the things we desire. Recognize when fear is controlling your thoughts. When we want the universe to hear what we are asking for, we don't want to be unclear. If we are focusing on fear that is what the universe will focus on as well.

- **Thoughts**—Thoughts are the driving force of the Law of Attraction. Everything that we manifest will first arise from our thoughts. They will incite the emotions we feel and influence our behaviors.

- **Imagination**—For the Law of Attraction to work in a way that benefits your life you need to tap into your imagination.

Visualization is a key practice in manifestation because it allows us to see, feel, and act on the things we want.

- **Belief/Expectancy**—Before you begin to manifest what you want, you need to let go of any disbelief you have in the process. You also need to release any doubt that you are worthy of or capable of receiving what you desire. Addressing your limiting beliefs and reshaping your thoughts will let you ask with authenticity and confidence for exactly what you deserve.

  Keep in mind, sometimes what we are asking for requires some harsh lessons. You may be expecting to attract the person of your dreams and when you think you have found them realize that they aren't everything you want in a relationship. Understand that the Law of Attraction will not only provide you with what you expect but will provide you with what you need.

- **Feelings/Vibration**—Manifestation will work better when you take time each day to focus on how you are feeling. Bring to your mind what you are asking for and draw your attention to how this will make you feel. Don't get pulled into how you are feeling now, this can often create feelings of lacking and fear, both of which will provide you with the opposite of what you want.

  Another way to ensure you attract more of what you want is to be in the moment. Focus on being more excited about the possibilities; focus on accepting that you already have within you the power to be who you want to become and live the life of your dreams. Shifting your feelings in the present moment from the negative to the positive is what will bring you more of the experiences and opportunities needed to generate more positive feelings.

- **Creative Attraction**—Manifestation will attract what you desire in life. We create the image of how we want to live our lives, what our days look like, and the things we want. Through this process of creating a visualization, we begin to attract and bring to reality what we imagine in our minds.

- **Inspired Action**—This is an area of manifestation that many misunderstand. Some will say that taking action on the things you desire will cause you not to manifest what you really want because it insinuates you have disbelief in the Universe's ability to make it happen. Simply visualizing and stating what you want is only the beginning of manifestation. When we begin to create a certain image of our lives, we naturally begin to align our behaviors, thoughts, and beliefs to this image. Inspired action occurs when we recognize all that we can accomplish, and begin to alter our lives in ways that make it possible for the Law of Attraction to work. For example, you cannot just ask the universe for more money if you are constantly spending and worried about paying bills. If you create a visualization of having enough money to support yourself, while also being able to indulge a little in what you enjoy, more details of how you achieve this come to light. Your visualization will not just be of someone handing you a bag of money. It will often include you finishing school, finding a better-paying job, starting your own business, or saving and creating a budget. From this more detailed visualization, you gain motivation, and you begin to take the steps that will lead you to attract more money. You might apply for different jobs or learn more about how to start a business. This is inspired action—you create the visualization and this gives you clarity on what you need to do; the Law of Attraction will provide you with the opportunities to receive what you ask for. This may appear to be a streak of luck, but behind-the-scenes you have been taking the right action that put you in the right place at the right time.

Manifestation energy is referred to as masculine or feminine. Understanding these two types of energies will help you with your manifestation practices. Many times people fail to recognize when they have a deficiency in one or both of these types of energy (Burnett, 2017). If there is a deficit it will be harder to manifest what you desire. This is when many people falsely believe that the Law of Attraction is not working in their favor.

Feminine Energy

Feminine energy is what will help you attract what you want. It works to support your intentions and clear away what blocks you from attracting what you try to manifest. Tapping into your feminine energy can elevate your ability to manifest all that you desire. Feminine energy is driven by what you are feeling in the present moment. When you focus your attention on feeling good, your feminine energy awakens and attracts to your life all that brings you joy.

Masculine Energy

Masculine energy guides you to act in ways that will attract what you desire. It is what puts you in the right place at the right time when opportunities arise. This energy is powerful in the sense that it provides you with what is needed for you to gain what you ask for in life.

Setting Intentions

Manifestation works by bringing to your life the energy that you give out through your thoughts and emotions. The things you want, the people who surround you, and the experiences you have lived through have all been guided to you through your energy field.

When you set intentions for manifestation it is important to focus on the result you want, not on the current problems in your life. When you focus your energy on what you don't want, that is what you will attract more of. When you constantly exhibit a negative emotion more experiences and situations will arise that increase these negative feelings. What you think and feel will work to bring to your life more of what causes these thoughts and feelings (Hoppe, n.d.).

The key to setting intentions is not just clarifying what it is you want, it is about establishing how it will make you feel when you receive it. What you feel will be the driving energy that attracts what you are asking for. Your intention needs to be specific. The more specific the better; the universe will understand and know exactly what you are asking for.

When you think about your intentions, don't just do this in passing. Make this a ritual. Dedicate time to sit down and become clear about what you want to attract more of. This should be a personal process and bring you into a relaxed mindset. When you are done with your intention setting, you should feel inspired. Intention setting can take many forms. A lot of people create a vision board when they set their intentions. They put a lot of time and thought into every element that is included in this board—they don't just throw something together. You do not need to create a vision board, but whatever you choose, make sure to treat your intentions with the same respect and importance.

Heart-Mind Synchronicity

When we manifest from the heart we cast out our energy with pure intention. Though our thoughts play a vital role in what we manifest, our hearts can have an even more powerful impact on what we attract. The heart is capable of producing 60 times more energy than the brain (Lopes, 2018). Our heart is what connects us to the Universe. While the mind can bring a lot of things to reality, it more often brings about the undesirable, since our thoughts can get away from us. The heart, however, is where our intuition lies. If we connect to our heart center when we manifest, we will not only give out higher vibration but will attract our deepest desires (Lopes, 2018). Connecting to the heart through heart-mind synchronicity can be done in a few simple steps. Though simple, these steps require practice to master—when you do you will find that your life changes drastically for the better.

Step one: We need to quiet the mind so that our hearts can be heard loud and clear. There is no one way to do this. Many practice meditation, while others find walking on the beach decreases the chatter in their head. The goal is to find an activity or practice that does not require mental energy and allows you to remain at peace in the moment.

Step two: Once you have turned down the volume on your thoughts, you can tune into what your heart speaks. To do this, you need to focus on the space in your chest that you feel the most love and kindness radiating from. When you see someone you love, you feel this radiating from your chest. This is the same space you want to tune into now.

Step three: This is one of the more challenging steps. This is when we become aware of the energy we are casting out from our hearts and minds. To become aware of this energy we need to become more alert and live in the present moment. This requires us to stop becoming caught up in the drama of our thoughts, the what-ifs, and should-dos. When we remain present and tuned into the loving space in our chest we will see how this energy radiates out of us and how it is cast into the world around us.

Step four: This final step brings our minds back into practice. The mind is still powerful, and since we are used to relying on it to make decisions for us, we need to allow it to assist our hearts to manifest our deepest desires. Listen to your heart and let your mind create the vision of your life based on what the heart speaks. The mind will conjure thoughts that align with the heart, but only if we let our hearts remain in control.

These four steps can be performed at any time. There is no need to wait until the perfect time. When you begin to allow your heart to take control of your experiences you will notice significant changes in your life.

Chapter 3: Love Thyself

Everything you attract in life will begin with what goes through your mind. We cannot begin to improve the way the Law of Attraction works in our life if we do not address what we are saying in our heads. The Law of Attraction can bring more love, happiness, and satisfaction to life, but only if we express love and gratitude for who we are.

Connecting With The Inner Self

To attract what we want, we need to align our desires with what we believe is possible, not with what we are lacking currently. This is a process that can be challenging to master. Many of us create visions of our lives and ask the universe for things because of our current situations. Most desires we crave emerge out of what we don't like. While we may best ask for more money, our focus will be on not having enough to pay bills or other things we wish we could buy but can't afford. We focus on what we believe will fix our problems and this, in turn, causes problems. This is because the problem we are trying to fix is not the real problem. You cannot cure loneliness by trying to manifest the ideal partner.

Relying on external forces to bring a solution will never solve the problem. We must learn to turn inward and listen to our thoughts and emotions—they will guide us to our deepest desire. Connecting to the heart is one way to bring more awareness to our own needs and wishes.

Personal Integrity

Integrity reveals itself when we are faced with obstacles in life. How we act in these moments has a significant influence on what we send out into the Universe. Acting with kindness, being helpful, and doing what is right are all positive actions that honor our personal integrity (Bidinger, n.d.).

Energy does not remain stagnant or stop flowing. Our energy, just as the energy flowing around us, is in constant motion. We are constantly expanding as our energy continues to flow beyond what is in our immediate surroundings.

Removing Blocks

A few things could be holding you back from attracting the right kind of people into your life. Your thoughts and internal dialogue can keep you in the same patterns that make it appear that you are unlucky in love.

Interrupting Patterns

If you have ever found yourself asking why you seem to get into the same relationships or have the same types of friends, it is because these are the people you are attracting to you. When you enter a relationship what do you tend to focus on most? The good qualities this person has or the bad? At the beginning of any relationship, we put blinders on and focus on the good qualities, while trying to ignore the bad. As time goes on, we shift from appreciating the good qualities to only seeing what we don't like in the other person. When the relationship ends we tell ourselves that we aren't ever going to get into a relationship with someone like that again. Focusing on what we don't want in a partner is what will continuously set us up for meeting more of those same people.

To attract the right partner, friends, or even improve on our current relationship, we need to let go of what we don't like and focus on the qualities we do. Additionally, these qualities are not just things we want other people to possess, they must also be qualities we see in ourselves. If you want to attract a loyal, loving partner that respects you, you first have to be a loyal and loving person who respects yourself. The way we treat ourselves is the way we will allow others to treat us. Attracting love begins by first loving yourself and transforming yourself into the type of person you wish to spend your life with. Partners may still come and go, but the relationship you have with yourself is one that will last the rest of your life. If you have a toxic relationship with yourself, all your other relationships will be toxic as well.

Belief Systems

Your beliefs about yourself and your ability to find love can be keeping you at a low level of vibrational energy. Recognizing these limiting beliefs is the first step to attracting the love you are seeking. Low self-esteem is a major contributor to many love blocks. Moments of self-doubt are expected. Occasional self-doubt is not the issue, nor is it what we need to address. It is when we continuously think that we are unworthy or incapable of finding love, and more importantly, loving ourselves, that we will continue to struggle in this area of our life.

The most common limiting belief system that many unintentionally hold include:

- Believing they are unloveable.
- Thinking they don't deserve to be loved.
- Fear of being hurt.
- An inability to be vulnerable.
- Fear of abandonment.
- Thinking it is up to someone else to make them happy.

What we believe is what will dictate what we attract. Any of these limiting beliefs will block the relationship we truly want.

Attracting Love

Attracting love requires us to build our self-esteem and fully embrace our imperfections. We are all imperfect in our own way; loving these imperfections will attract the right person who will love them, too. Get into the habit of telling yourself daily what you love about yourself. Find the unique qualities that allow you to stand out. When someone gives you a compliment, say "thank you". When we feel unworthy of love we have a habit of feeling embarrassed or as if the person complimenting us is lying. This does nothing to build our confidence or counter the limiting beliefs we have.

Be kind to yourself and practice self-compassion. No matter what relationships you have had in the past, ruminating over them will not change the next one; instead, it sets you up to repeat the same experiences. When we are kind to ourselves, forgive ourselves, and permit ourselves to heal from past hurt, we will be better prepared for the love that the Universe sends our way.

Once we have allowed ourselves to heal from past relationships we need to be clear about what we will allow for our future relationships. Establishing boundaries is necessary for all areas of your life, but especially when it comes to how we allow others to treat us. This stems from how we treat ourselves. When we see our own self-worth, there is less chance of us tolerating someone else tearing that down. You will naturally set up boundaries, not to block people out, but to establish trust with yourself that you will not tolerate certain behaviors or treatment from others. Boundaries are essential for finding the right relationship and friendships. Without boundaries, we will let others take advantage of us and this just leads us back to where we started, feeling unloved and unlovable.

Finally, have patience. Finding the right person is not something you want to rush. The Universe is working to align you with the people who will add value to your life. You need to see your own value first—love yourself first. Only then will you be ready to accept this from another.

Chapter 4: Abundance is All Around You

Next to love, money is one of the most common things that people want more of. Money, however, is only a small factor that contributes to living a life of abundance. When we speak of abundance we are not just referring to material wealth. Abundance refers to everything that we acquire that satisfies our needs and our wants. It is about having more than enough money, friendships, opportunities, interests, and health to live a fulfilling life. Though you may be looking to attract more money using the Law of Attraction understand that what you tend to ask for is not financial freedom, but instead, are things that keep you in a lacking state of mind.

Scarcity Mindset

If you don't think you have enough you will not receive more. Most people have a resistance to attracting abundance because they focus on the stress, frustration, and disappointments that create their lacking mindset.

A scarcity mindset will always keep abundance flowing away from you. You may even notice that the more you try to manifest abundance the more it seems to be flowing to those around you. This is typically due to comparing what you have to what others have. You see someone with the money, house, car, and vacation you want and think "they have more than enough, they have everything I am trying to attract"; in turn, all that energy is flowing towards them and is working to bring them more of what you are jealous of.

Remember, where we focus our attention is where our energy will go, and that is what we receive in return. If you spend your time focusing only on what others have you will be sending them more—not yourself.

Delicate Balance

If you dream of an abundant life you have to shift your mindset. Wanting more out of life is not a bad thing, but this want of more often results in feelings of desperation. This lowers your frequencies and causes you to push away the things that you are searching for. Maintain a balance of feeling grateful for all that you have, while remaining patient and content in knowing that all that you desire is coming your way.

This is the Law of Paradoxical Intent. It is the process of appreciating all that you have while shifting to a mindset that brings you joy when working towards the other things you wish to gain. The delicate aspect of this is when we set goals for ourselves to achieve more they often make us anxious. We become too wrapped up in having to accomplish them. We create a belief around the idea that if we just do this one thing then we will be satisfied. Desperation arises and soon we are obsessed with chasing after the next thing.

Abundance will only flow into your life when you maintain satisfaction in all that you have. Being able to find joy in the things that you already possess. There is nothing wrong with thinking ahead to the future, but if we do not enjoy all that we have in the present, then our future will never change.

Process Creation

If you have struggled to bring abundance into your life you are trying to force it too much. You already have what you need in life, but you are not living in alignment with this truth. We create our own reality—if you look at your environment or where you are at now in your life and are filled with regret, anxiety, or despair, then you will only be abundant in these negative feelings. If instead, you look around you and are grateful for all that you see, for all that you are working towards, and begin to live according to the fact that you have everything you need, then your life will be filled with more enjoyable abundance.

You need to live as though you have already received what you are asking for. If you are asking for money act as though you already have it, that it is sitting in your bank account. What will you do with it? Vacation? Buy a car? If you do not already envision what changes will come when the money comes, then you are resisting it. If you cannot visualize the joy you will gain from having this wealth and feel that joy in the present, you will never experience it.

The universe has already provided you with what you have asked for. Not having enough money easily stirs up negative emotions. We want to stir up positive feelings.

Release

If you keep yourself cluttered both mentally and physically, you will not have room for more. Letting go of the things that we have in excess will welcome more of what we desire. To attract abundance we need to make room in our lives for more. This doesn't just relate to physical things that you may have been holding on to for too long. Releasing is a process of letting go of all that does not serve you.

When you release, you strengthen your trust and belief in knowing that what you are asking for is on its way. Letting go of doubts, fears, and thoughts is the only way you will make room for the abundance you wish for. This requires one to let go of old behaviors and systems so that new, successful ones can take up space. When we release these unwanted and unhelpful components, change can begin to happen.

Attracting Wealth

The meaning of wealth differs from person to person. When trying to manifest abundance we need to clearly define what it means to us and what an abundant life looks like. Once we have established this understanding we need to look closely at the relationship we have with money. The right relationship will always provide you with what you need, the wrong one will keep you in scarcity. To have a good relationship with money we need to look at what exactly we think about money. You may be telling the universe that you have enough money so that you can attract more, but even the smallest thought about needing more is going to keep you stuck. Consider how you feel about your financial situation right now. Is it frustrating? Will just a little more money solve your problems? Do you think of your job as never supplying you with enough? Are you constantly making lacking statements about how you can't afford things? All these indicate a poor relationship with money.

To have a good relationship with money, and to allow the Law of Attraction to work in your favor in this area, you need to shift your thinking. You don't need more money because you already have enough. If you want to allow more money to flow into your life you need to have a positive relationship with money. You appreciate all that you have and are grateful for all the streams it currently arrives to you through. You do not fear or question how you will pay bills or feel resentment when you don't buy something because of the cost.

Money will only flow freely to your life when you let go of the resistance you have. Resistance makes you feel frustrated, stressed, and desperate (Attracting abundance and allowing abundance, n.d.). Recognizing when there is resistance will help you improve how you feel about your financial situation.

Law of Attraction for Success

The Law of Attraction is not just about thinking or stating what you want. It is about embracing the things that we really want out of life. When we do this, we do not just send wishes out into the universe, we take action. When what we think becomes what we believe, we will adjust our daily actions to align with those beliefs. This is where the Law of Attraction comes into effect.

If we are acting as if we already possess the things we desire, or act as though they will manifest soon, the universe provides us with the right opportunities to gain these things. This is how many successful individuals like Oprah, Will Smith, Tony Robbins, and Denzel

Washington have stayed on course to attract all that they have in life. They have a deep understanding that their thoughts, emotions, and views of the world around them will greatly impact what they receive in life. The main thing to point out is that they did not just wish their success into being. They fully believed that what they wanted to achieve was possible and despite not knowing how to make these things happen they began taking action. Even if they may have taken action on the wrong things some of the time this action nonetheless is what led to greater opportunities.

A life of abundance can be gained when we see clearly that we already possess everything we need to reach the level of success we desire. We just have to learn to trust the process and maintain the belief in ourselves and what we are doing. You won't see significant changes overnight, but you know that change is on the way if you are consistent.

Chapter 5: Healthy Mind, Healthy Body, Healthy Life

A healthy life is one that keeps us full of energy. When we feel comfortable in our bodies we send out more positive vibrations. Being grateful for all that we can do begins to bring good health to our life. Mastering our emotions is how we attract optimal health.

One thing to note—this chapter is not about providing medical treatments to cure health conditions. Though we can tap into the powers of the Law of Attraction to live a healthier life, this in no way means you shouldn't see a doctor when you are ill.

Emotional Manifestation

It is true that what you feel and think will attract whatever will cause more of those things. Many misinterpret this to mean they have to be happy and joyous all the time. Emotions all have their time and place; many cause us to avoid dangers and will guide us to uncover truths we would otherwise miss. You don't want to cover up or avoid negative emotions. Neglecting these emotions does not lead to more happiness, it leads to more unpleasant feelings. The only way to clear negative emotions and thoughts from the mind is to let them run their course and address the root cause of them. Only if we address these negative emotions will we uncover the message they are sending us.

Negative emotions are not meant to be ignored, they are to be used as a tool to dig deeper into what we want in life. Negative emotions are not meant to be manipulated, just as we don't want to manipulate the positive ones. They can be worked through to bring you to an authentic place of peace and contentment.

Shifting from Negative to Positive Emotions

The first step to manifest what you want in life is to understand how your negative emotions and thoughts are keeping you stuck in a life you don't enjoy (Western Wellness Team, 2014). Think about how negative emotions instantly affect your day. For instance, you wake up late and rush to get to work. You are already filled with anxiety about getting to work on time. You make careless mistakes. You spill coffee on your shirt and have to rush to change before leaving—causing you to be even later. This adds to the negative emotions. As you drive to work, you get stuck in traffic, and more unpleasant emotions arise in the form of frustration, rage, and impatience. When you get to work you snap at your coworkers, which you instantly regret, stirring up more negative emotions. And this is how your day continues until you get back at home and decide to relieve all your stress in front of the television eating the most convenient thing you can grab, which also happens to be the unhealthiest.

As you can see, our negative emotions will immediately cause a chain reaction of more negative events. Now, consider how this works on a much larger scale when we add in the Law of Attraction. This one day has sent out millions of negative vibes, and the universe responds by giving back what you send out. It may not affect you instantly, but weeks later you miss a huge promotion, or lose your job, or get hit with a huge financial blow that throws your life off the intended course.

If, however, we remain in control of our emotions and shift them from negative to positive we not only avoid bad days like this but keep our energy vibration at a high level so we attract more of the good things. Unfortunately, we think this is much harder than it has to be. Shifting our negative thoughts is a simple matter of pausing and breathing before we react. In the moment, when our emotions are running wild, this feels impossible to do. If we learn to just pause before we react to our emotions, we stay in check and we can act in more productive and positive ways.

Stress Influence on Our Energy

Stress is a normal part of life. A little bit of stress here and there will not throw off your vibrations or undo all the work you have been putting into manifesting your deepest desires. Stress, however, can cause serious turmoil with our health, which the Law of Attraction cannot undo. When we are stressed we can not see clearly all that we have and should be grateful for now. It keeps us in a lacking mentality full of fear and disbelief.

It is pertinent that you use effective techniques to combat high levels of stress. Some suggestions include:

- Meditation
- Yoga
- Journaling
- Affirmation

Stress also draws us off our energy. When we are stressed the body needs to work harder to function properly. This is energy that could be better used to work towards the other things that we desire. Not only does this mean we physically do not have the energy to function, but the energy we release to the universe is low.

The Law of Allowing

The Law of Allowing is a complex practice, but is where you will learn how to let your positive thoughts guide you. You don't need to take control of everything happening in your life but simply feel confident that the universe is leading you in the right direction.

When we use phrases that include "I cannot" or "I am not", we are fighting an uphill battle. This disbelief is what will keep you stuck having the same experiences you don't want to have and receiving the things that do not serve you.

The Law of Allowing boils down to giving yourself permission to experience and have all that you desire. It also brings to focus how we must do the same for others. When we encounter someone who does not agree with us or has different opinions, our initial reaction is to focus on what we don't agree with. This, in turn, begins to shift the flow of energy. You are no longer attracting what you want, but attracting what you don't want.

Learning to let others be and do as they want will give you the freedom to manifest what you want. Letting things just be as they are, without judgment, fear, or dissatisfaction, will bring you peace. There are many things that we cannot control, but we tend to focus a lot of attention and energy on these things. What is your first reaction when you hear news of a tragic occurrence? You might instantly feel sorrow—you feel bad for the people affected or those who are suffering. This only sends out more sadness and despair. This is not to say you cannot feel empathy, you don't want to think that their suffering is a good thing. You do, however, need to focus on sending out love and peace to those affected. Understanding that you cannot control most situations, other people, or natural occurrences can help you control your reaction to hearing about devastation.

Say "Yes" to What You Want

If you focus in any way on the things that you do not want you will unintentionally attract them into your life. As we pointed out earlier, if we focus our attention on what others have we will shift our energy to create more of that for them. We also unintentionally attract these things into our life. The Law of Attraction is not just about creating more of what we desire in our lives; it is about understanding that our energy affects those around us. If we want more for ourselves we need to accept and encourage others to have more in theirs.

Allowing ourselves and others to receive what we desire lies in our ability to say yes. Saying "yes", you attract more of what you receive. When you say "no", you receive more of what you are trying to reject. When more of this flows into your life the natural reaction is to push back more, and as a result, you receive more. The Law of Allowing will help you accept that what others want is ok for them, even if you do not agree. You do not need to say no to the things that they want more of, and saying no is necessary some of the time. You cannot say yes to everything, but you can say no in a way that makes it clear that you are saying no because of a greater desire.

Inspired action is a core principle of the Law of Allowing. When we set an intention we want to focus on what we want, not how to get it. The universe will supply the how—the what is up to you to define. Inspired actions are those that align with your vision. Each action you take has been perfectly presented to you so that receiving all that you want in life comes naturally.

Transcendental Meditation

Relax the mind, relax the body, and then you can focus on attracting more of what you desire. The real "secret' to the Law of Attraction is meditation. Receiving what you want from the universe requires significant mind control. When we are able to control our thoughts, emotions, and internal dialogue, everything else will begin to naturally fall into place. While it may appear simple enough, meditation is not something that most can conquer.

Meditation is a technique that takes practice and patience. There is no one perfect way to meditate to improve how the Law of Attraction benefits your life. Meditation comes in many forms, falling into one of two categories: transcendental or concentrative. Both of these categories have multiple techniques and approaches. The more you commit to meditation, the easier the process becomes and the more profound the impact you will experience.

Transcendental meditation is a unique meditation technique. This practice is taught by a licensed instructor. This meditation does require more commitment. You are recommended to practice twice a day for 20 minutes, once in the morning and once in the late afternoon. Each session should be guided by an instructor. The instructor works with you to create a personal mantra, which you repeat during each meditation session. The instructor guides you to stay aligned with the mantra, as this is the saying that will guide your thoughts.

This doesn't mean that other forms of meditation should not be considered. Though transcendental meditation can align you with universal power and opens you to embracing and attracting what you desire in life, all forms of meditation will lead you to a path of peace and satisfaction.

Chapter 6: Attracting Your Dream Life

Once fully understood, the Law of Attraction can transform your life. When you first begin your journey with the practices and lessons of the Law of Attraction you may feel the need to limit what you ask for. If you are hesitant to ask for more because of disbelief, then you will not benefit from the Law of Attraction in the way you hope. If you fully embrace the possibilities and welcome the changes that are coming your way, you will find that the life you have always dreamed of is the life you are living right now. This is important to remember. The reality is that the life we are living is the one we have already visualized for ourselves, whether we have done it intentionally or not. Your dream life is already playing out, but your perspective and how you are experiencing it is what makes you feel like it is lacking. In this chapter, we will discuss how to optimize the Law of Attraction so you can live this dream life every day.

Focused Visualization

Dream big. What you ask for may seem impossible right now, but consider how amazing it would be if these things actually manifested. Don't limit yourself to what you think is possible now, allow yourself to think about the future. How will you be living a year from now, three years from now, five or ten years from now? Looking forward and seeing the possibilities that lay ahead can jumpstart the process of attracting these things sooner rather than later. Get creative with what you see for yourself. Nothing is out of reach—remember, you create your own reality.

Visualization is a powerful tool to not only aid in shifting the way the Law of Attraction works for you but accelerating it. When we use visualization we (Canfield, n.d.):

- Activate the creative subconscious.
- Become more aware of what we already possess so we can receive what we ask for.
- Begin to attract what we need to accomplish a goal.

- Increase our intrinsic motivation.

We can use visualization to achieve our biggest goals and reach our full potential. This practice is best performed after you wake in the morning, after meditating, or just before you go to bed. You want to be in your most relaxed state. Once in your relaxed state, follow the steps below.

Step one: First, you will visualize yourself accomplishing what you want to achieve. See yourself as if you are watching a movie, or perhaps an audience member of a live event. The movie you are watching or the performance you are witnessing is of yourself accomplish the goal you have set. See yourself perfectly doing what you need to do to accomplish each step in your goal achievement process. What do you need to do first? Witness yourself completing the task in as much detail as possible. What are you wearing? What are your surroundings? What does your facial expression show? What do you hear? Bring as much detail to the movie or performance as possible. Once you have all the details, hone in on what you feel as you do what you need to do.

Step two: Now you are going to shift from being a bystander to an actual part of the movie. See yourself getting up and walking up to the movie screen, or approaching the stage, where you witnessed yourself accomplishing your desire. Become a part of the movie; replay the whole scene you witnessed in the previous step, but instead of just watching, you are now the leading character. Go through the experience—seeing things from your own perspective. See all the details you noticed in the previous step but from your own eyes.

Step three: Finally, we want to make this picture a physical part of us. Once you have placed yourself in the movie or performance, both as a bystander and the main performer, and have seen what it feels like to accomplish what you want, you will exit the movie or stage and return to where you were at the beginning. The movie (or performance of yourself) is still playing. Imagine the screen or stage getting smaller. Pick up and hold the screen or stage in your hand as it gets even smaller. Once it is a bite-sized piece, bring it to your mouth and swallow it. Visualize this screen traveling down to your stomach, where it breaks down to the smallest particles and is released into your bloodstream. Imagine these particles spreading throughout your body, awakening every cell and aligning your whole being with that picture of you accomplishing what you want.

Affirming Your Desires

Affirmations can be used throughout your day to keep you focused on what you want to achieve. They are not statements made to counter what you don't want. "I am not going to spend any money." " I am not getting sick." These do not affirm what you want; they focus on what you don't want.

An affirmation can be a powerful tool to shift your mindset, rewire your thinking, and create belief in what you want to occur in your life. Many use them in the wrong way by telling themselves phrases over and over that don't resonate, or that deep down they don't believe. Affirmations are not just words you say to yourself to feel better, "I am a successful business person." They are statements that clearly define what we want to feel because of what we have or because of who we are. "I am in love with the life I am living." "I am happy and healthy." "I am grateful for all the caring people in my life." These statements do not just focus on what we want, they focus on how living that life will make us feel. This is how affirmation can be used to help manifest our dream life.

Positive Affirmations

Creating positive affirmations takes some thought and deep consideration. If we do not clearly state what we desire we will ultimately receive that which we don't. When you create a positive affirmation, it should strengthen the feeling of expressing the phrase. The more specific you are with your affirmation the easier it is for the universe to deliver what you ask for. For example, a good affirmation to start with may state "I am happy and living a healthy life." A more specific affirmation will state, "My body is in optimal health, my heart is strong, my lungs are clear, and my immune system is in prime condition." This is specific and when you say a statement like this you will feel healthier and stronger.

Here are some additional tips to create positive affirmations:

1. You have to fully believe what you are saying. Positive affirmations make you feel hopeful, calm, empowered, and happy. If you do not believe what you are affirming, then you will feel foolish, frustrated, and fearful. No matter how often you repeat them, if you don't believe what you say there is no point in saying them.
2. Your affirmation should directly reflect your goals and combat negative thoughts.
3. Create affirmations that specifically target limiting beliefs or negative thoughts that run through your mind frequently.
4. Combine your affirmation with your visualizations; your visualization can serve as a guide to uncover the right affirmation that works best for you.
5. Affirmations must be positive.
6. Phrase your affirmation as if what you are speaking of has already come to be.

Creating the Perfect Present

Shift your mindset to make the best out of every situation. Even when we notice that the Law of Attraction is working in our favor, unforeseen circumstances will arise. There are always going to be struggles to overcome because we cannot control everything that happens around us. In these moments it is vital that we remain positive and find the silver lining. If we shift our mindset to one that makes us the victim, we will only experience more suffering. Learning to remain in the present moment, and maintain hope and optimism, ensures that we stay aligned with the positive vibrations that we may not as easily notice.

The present moment is always the perfect moment. If we look at all that is wrong in our life we are not living in the present. Worrying about what will happen in the future takes us out of the present moment. Reliving past events and tormenting ourselves with regret and resentment removes us from the present moment. The Law of Attraction is at work now—in this moment—and at any moment your energy can change and shift the course of your life. Staying present and enjoying each moment as it unfolds is what will allow us to see opportunities when they are present to us.

Let Your Emotions Guide You

Joy, happiness, and living with purpose lead to expansion. Accept that each thought and emotion sets the stage for what will manifest in your life. Our thoughts and emotions are like seeds. Each one is planted and will grow what we have wished for. Every reaction we have will water these seeds and as they bloom they will either bear what we desire or what we are trying to repel.

Emotions should be our guiding light that leads us to the things that we want, not just saying what we want. We can say we want a million dollars but if our inner voice tells us we are not worthy and our emotions are wrought with fear, those millions will never come. In addition to this conflict, the money may not be what we are truly seeking. What does that million dollars actually mean? Financial security? More quality time with the family? These inner desires are what we are really asking for. The money is just a quick solution. The energy we give out will reflect that—and the millions may never come—because we are more likely to be presented with opportunities that allow us that financial freedom or quality time.

When we understand that this is how the Law of Attraction works we become more aware and mindful of what we are thinking and feeling. We intentionally find truth to counter negative thoughts, we utilize affirmation to shift our energy, and we react to negativity in a way that sheds light on every situation. This doesn't mean that things are always pleasant, it simply means we do not let these unpleasantries keep us stuck.

Allow your emotions to guide where you go. When we are happy and enjoying what we do we are expanding. These feelings indicate that we are on the right path. Negative feelings cause us to feel powerless and uncertain. These indicate that the direction we are going is not in alignment with what we want.

Conclusion

The Law of Attraction is a powerful concept. It makes you responsible for the life you decide to live. Understanding that everything that has come to you has been the result of the choices you have made is no easy truth to accept. Many of the things we experience in life we do not intentionally ask for, and some we have no control or power over. But what we do control and have a say in is how we live our lives, the happiness we experience, and how satisfied we are in our day. If something in your life is not meeting your expectations or providing you with the happiness you desire, you can at any moment choose a different direction.

When you choose to embrace and believe in what is possible, the impossible begins to happen. When you decide to ask for what you want from the universe, you will receive what you ask for. The Law of Attraction may be powerful, but it all comes down to your choice. Do you choose to be optimistic or pessimistic? Do you choose to see life with a fresh and positive perspective or from a tainted view of the past?

This book has provided you with information that does not just tell you what the Law of Attraction is or what it does. You have learned how to implement simple changes, make more positive choices, and begin to attract what you want more of in your life.

Whether you are looking to gain wealth, success, find love, or improve your health, you have the ability to create all that you desire. All that you have, and all that you will have, manifests out of where you focus your attention. Remember—you are the creator of your life. You are responsible for what you allow to enter into your life; everything that comes is a result of your own thoughts and emotions. I hope that you have found clarity in these pages. I hope that you have begun to take the first steps to manifest the life of your dreams and that you have already begun to feel the benefits from these first steps.

I hope that you continue to make progress and experience all that the Universe has to offer.

References

Attracting abundance and allowing abundance. (n.d.). Wings for the Heart. http://wingsfortheheart.com/abundance-prosperity/attracting-abundance-allowing-abundance/

Bernstein, G. (2021, January 27). *5 Tips to manifest miracles*. Mind Body Green. https://www.mindbodygreen.com/0-9033/5-tips-to-manifest-miracles.html

Bidinger, S. (n.d.). *The 7 Laws Of Attraction*. Transformation Seeker's Guide. https://www.practical-personal-development-advice.com/7-laws-of-attraction.html

Brown, J., & Wong, J. (2017, June 6). *How gratitude changes you and your brain*. Greater Good. https://greatergood.berkeley.edu/article/item/how_gratitude_changes_you_and_your_brain

Burnett, L. (2017, October 11). *Do you know your core manifestation energy?* LloydBurnett.com. https://www.lloydburnett.com/blog/3009-do-you-know-your-core-manifestation

Canfield, J. (n.d.). *Visualization techniques to manifest desired outcomes*. Jack Canfield Maximizing Your Potential. https://www.jackcanfield.com/blog/visualize-and-affirm-your-desired-outcomes-a-step-by-step-guide/

Cooper, K. (2016, January 27). *Law of Attraction: 4 Ways you're derailing deliberate creation*. HuffPost. https://www.huffpost.com/entry/law-of-attraction-4-ways-youre-derailing-deliberate-creation_b_9083582

Ester. (n.d.). *The 6 most common love blocks and how to clear them*. Through the Phases. https://www.throughthephases.com/love-blocks/

Gallagher, V. M. (2019). *Practical law of attraction: Align yourself with the manifesting conditions and successfully attract your desires*. Victoria M. Gallagher.

Hart, H. (n.d.). *A powerful feminine energy secret to manifesting anything you want*. Attract the One. https://attracttheone.com/law-of-attraction/a-powerful-feminine-energy-secret-to-manifesting-anything-you-want/

Hoppe, C. (n.d.). *Manifestation skills*. University of Metaphysical Sciences. https://metaphysicsuniversity.com/manifestation-skills-excerpt/

Hurst, K. (n.d.). *Law Of Attraction history: The origins of the law of attraction uncovered*. The Law of Attraction. https://www.thelawofattraction.com/history-law-attraction-uncovered/

Law of Attraction. (n.d.). Eco Institute. https://eocinstitute.org/meditation/law-of-attraction/?n_bld

Lopes, C. (2018, June 16). *The 4-step Process for using your heart to manifest your ideal life*. Christina Lopes. https://christina-lopes.com/blog/spirituality/the-4-step-process-for-using-your-heart-to-manifest-your-ideal-life/

The Law of Attraction Q & A: What is the Art of Allowing. (n.d.). Www.real-Life-Law-of-Attraction.com. https://www.real-life-law-of-attraction.com/art-of-allowing.html

Western Wellness Team. (2014, September 22). *Manifesting perfect health*. Www.westernwellness.com.au. https://www.westernwellness.com.au/blog/2014/09/manifesting-perfect-health.html#:~:text=The%20law%20of%20attraction%20applied

Manifesting – Beginners Guide

Manifestation Strategies to Achieve Your Desires for Money, Love, Abundance, Happiness, and Success to Become Your Greatest Self

Olivia Clifford

Introduction

Lao Tzu once asserted that "A journey of a thousand miles begins with a single step" (Literary Devices, 2019). There is some immense truth to this statement as we look toward achieving what we want in life. Undeniably, there is a lot that we demand in life. In fact, true happiness, love, abundance, and all our heart's desires are governed by the achievements we make. How great can life be if only you had faith in the first step you take. To get to your destination, you don't have to worry about how you will get there. Rather, you only need to believe in yourself and take the first step. This is what the power of manifesting is all about - Faith in the unseen.

When you stop to reflect on your life and the things you desire for yourself, chances are you fill your mind and heart with worry and anxiety. We often stress ourselves because we think that our goals are too far-fetched. Worse, we even believe that we are walking down the wrong path in life. But the truth of the matter is that the universe always delivers. The universe always gifts us with what we want if only we ask in the right manner. The phrase, "Ask and it will be given to you; seek and you will find; knock, and the door will be opened to you,", is not new to most of us (Bible Hub, 2021). We're always hopeful for tomorrow because we believe that we would achieve something we had planned. So, why is it so difficult to believe that you can manifest what you want into your life?

Maybe you're thinking of manifesting abundance, money, wealth, love, fruitful relationships, and a great career. It doesn't matter what you want to manifest; the most important thing is for you to believe with conviction that it's possible. Manifesting – Beginners Guide will reveal what you need to do to start practicing how to attract what you want into your life. It's a well-known fact that you're what you think about most of the time. Consequently, by aligning your thoughts to the things you desire, there is no doubt that, sooner or later, you will live your best life.

That said, one of the main keys that will guarantee you manifest what you want into your life is – the law of attraction. This is one of the laws of the universe that will guide you in bringing what you want into your life. It's a simple law that will shape your life in ways you never imagined before. All you have to do is to determine what you want in life and go for it.

Think about living the life of your dreams. Keep in mind that one of the most crucial things you need to work on as you use this guide to learn more about manifesting strategies is your belief system. There is nothing that is beyond your reach if you truly believe in yourself. That's how the universe works. When great things start manifesting into your life, you will be amazed as the universe's energies work life's magic. So, ask in the right way, seek in the right direction, and knock on the right doors. When this happens, you will live a life full of abundance and joy.

Start developing an abundance mindset as you read this book. Take a moment to connect with your higher self. Allow positive, fulfilling thoughts to fill your mind. There is nothing you lack in this world. You are enough, and that you have enough. Take a look around you and express gratitude for the things you already have. Life didn't just happen by chance. You deserve what you have, and you have the ability to attract more into your life. Be confident in yourself and the path you're about to take into a whole new world full of abundance.

Before we begin, have it in mind that manifesting what you want in life isn't about asking the universe and expecting things to happen. You need to take a bold step and take action on your goals and dreams. Action is what is required from you. It's vital that you surround yourself with energies that are in line with what you want. Manifesting isn't a passive exercise. Fortunately, once you develop the right habits that attract what you want in life, everything else will fall into place. So, don't be discouraged.

Let's begin!

Chapter 1: The Law of Attraction

Just like the law of gravity, the law of attraction is always in action. Believe it or not, one of the main keys to manifesting what you want in life is by understanding that there is energy in you. It's essential to cultivate the energy within you to attract what you want in life. You've often heard that you create the life you want. Well, this is true. You're always creating the reality that you call life every day. This happens through your thoughts, whether consciously or subconsciously.

The law of attraction applies to your life in many ways. Change your thoughts for a moment, and you will be happy or sad, depending on the direction of your thoughts. For instance, think of an experience that changed your life in the past. When you immerse yourself in the positive thought, chances are you will find yourself smiling. Now, think of a painful experience that you rarely want to be associated with. There is nothing worth smiling about with such negative thoughts. Consequently, you might feel weary just at the thought of it. What this means is that you can change how you feel by simply changing your thoughts. This is how you create reality in your everyday life.

In the same way, you can start manifesting what you want into your life by leveraging the law of attraction. This law will change your life by the simple fact that you will be more conscious of how and what you think about most of the time. In other words, you will be more in control of your life.

One amazing thing about the law of attraction is that it will introduce you to a world full of miracles. It gives you an opportunity to see past the impossibilities that might have been holding you back. Once you master this law, it would be easy for you to challenge the scarcity mindset that often deters people from succeeding and achieving their goals.

What Is the Law of Attraction?

Put it simply, the law of attraction indicates that you attract the life you want by focusing on the things you would want in your life. This can also be understood in the form of - energy flows where attention goes. With this in mind, the most important thing you need to focus on is to determine what you want in life. Ask yourself - "What do I really want?" This is an important question that would ensure you know where to focus your energy. Ideally, this is what intentional living is all about.

Strive to focus on the positive things in life, and good things will manifest in your path. Make a list of the things you would wish to accomplish. Create positive affirmations around your goals. Suppose you continuously affirm to yourself that you're great or that you're wealthy and blessed. In that case, the universe will sync with your positive energies.

On the contrary, if you focus on things you lack, this will only evoke negative emotions. When this happens, negativity will haunt you like a plague. Ever wondered why a series of bad events might happen in your life when you focus on how life is not working out for you? Well, this is one way in which the law of attraction works.

When you're feeling enthusiastic, excited, happy, and appreciative of how life is good to you, you send out positive vibes. Interestingly, good things will continue manifesting in your path. This means that you can learn and master how to leverage the law of attraction at all times. Of course, this is not easy, especially when you're going through a difficult time. But the law of attraction works like magic. Your life can quickly transform right before your eyes, and you would be surprised with how life happens for you.

The following are three fundamental tenets of the law of attraction.

You Are the Creator

The law of attraction is based on the simple principle that life doesn't just happen. You're the creator of the reality that manifests in your life. No one but you is responsible for your life. You have control over the experiences that you go through in life. The people you interact with, the friends you have, the amount of money you get, your level of happiness, etc. It sounds crazy, but it's true. Understanding the power you have over your life comes with the revelation that you're not a victim in life. Rather, life happens for you - just as you want it. Amazing, right?

When you finally understand how the law of attraction works, you enter into a realm where you use your mind to shape your life. A change of thought is all you need to start looking at challenges from a positive perspective. What's more, you will begin to live abundantly because you know there is power within you to change your life without allowing self-limiting doubts to get the best of you. Therefore, you're always creating your life. Nothing should stop you from creating a life you fancy. Just take the first step, as Lao Tzu mentioned in his quote regarding taking the first step in your journey of a thousand miles.

Still skeptical about how you can attract what you want into your life? Well, let's consider how you can use the law of attraction to manifest money.

Given the opportunity, we all would want to live abundantly by accumulating more wealth. But one of the biggest challenges most people face is that they have a poor relationship with money. This prevents them from fully accomplishing their goals and living the life they've always wanted. Manifesting money starts in the mind. Most individuals find it challenging to think positively about money because of their negative belief system.

The law of attraction comes in to help you change your belief system. This is what you need to start thinking of prosperity and amassing the wealth you need into your life. However, for this to work, you must take action and put the law into practice.

Start identifying some of the limiting beliefs you have about money. For instance, growing up, we were made to believe that money is the root of all evil or that money doesn't grow on trees, or money can't buy you happiness. These are examples of limiting beliefs that influence you to think negatively about money. It's crucial to see money as a tool that will help you make your dreams a reality. More importantly, money is accessible, and it's available in unlimited supply. With this mentality, it's easier for you to work toward manifesting wealth in your life.

The law of attraction also works through the power of visualization. Whatever you're thinking of acquiring into your life, you need to think like you already have it. For instance, visualize having enough money that you don't have to go from paycheck to paycheck trying to make ends meet. Think of financial freedom and how it can give you an opportunity to follow your passion without the need to get paid for it. Once you develop this picture in your mind, act like it. Act like you already have the amount of money you need. How would your life change? Live like you're wealthy, and the universe will listen to you through your thoughts and emotions. The point here is that visualization helps to create an abundance mindset. And everything else works like magic to ensure you live a fulfilling life.

Thoughts Become Things

The law of attraction is also based on the principle that your thoughts act as magnets. Basically, you are what you think about, which means that you can change your life by changing your thoughts. The idea here is that you should raise your awareness of your thoughts. If you're constantly thinking of good things, you increase the chances of great things happening in your life. The best part is that you can easily shift your thoughts even when you're not thinking positively. By making conscious efforts to take control of your thoughts, you also evoke positive vibes that attract good things your way.

You Attract What You Give Attention To

Like attracts like. And in the same, the energy goes where the attention flows. It's that simple. The law of attraction indicates that you attract everything that you pay attention to. The worst mistake we often make in life is that we tend to focus more on the things we don't want. The problem with this style of thinking is that we attract negativity. So, people who often dread going broke will find themselves struggling with their finances. The same case applies to relationships and other facets of your life.

When putting the law of attraction into practice, consider asking the universe for what you want. Stop thinking about what you don't want. If you're going to succeed in your career, focus more on what it takes for you to succeed. Strive to live intentionally. By doing this, you will start living a fulfilling life. Things will fall into place, not because you're working extra hard, but because your energies are in line with what you want.

With regards to your relationships, if you're looking to create a life full of love, focus on exuding love to the people around you. Be the love that you wish to attract. Put yourself first and practice self-love. Take care of yourself so you can be in a better position to help those around you. Learn to express gratitude for the fruitful relationships you share with others. This is how you create a sense of abundance around you.

The law of attraction is easy to think about but difficult to implement. Why? Because people allow themselves to fall prey to negative bias. Human beings are hardwired to think negatively. This means that it's easy for you to think of the worst that might happen to you compared to thinking of greatness and abundance. Leverage the power vested in you to attract the life you want. You don't have to wait any longer to start manifesting love, bliss, money, abundance, and success into your life. Start taking small baby steps in the right direction. This can be as simple as changing your thoughts.

Chapter 2: The Power of Now

There is no reason to think that life can be free from pain and sorrow. The best thing you can do to overcome challenges in your path is to learn to live with them. And the worst thing you should think of doing is to try and avoid them. Doing this will only cause you more pain and sorrow. Why? Because you will fight a losing battle, and that's where life seems unbearable.

However, most of the pains and sorrow we experience are self-inflicted. Usually, this happens when we allow our minds to run our lives. The pain most people go through comes in the form of nonacceptance or some sort of resistance to how life has transitioned. Perhaps you might be too judgmental to appreciate the importance of change in your life. When this happens, negativity creeps in, and you would conclude that life is not fair. The mind always strives to escape from the present moment. The more you associate with your mind, the more likely you will suffer. On the contrary, if you can accept to live in the NOW, you can easily free yourself from pain and your egoic mind.

The mind always seeks to run the show. We should understand here that when the mind is in control, you will rarely live in the present moment. You will find yourself either living in the past or the future. In other words, your true nature becomes shadowed by the mind. To separate yourself from the mind, you should realize that you only have NOW to change and live a happy and blissful life. This means saying 'yes' to the present moment at all times. Why try to oppose the flow of life and expect to be happy? Just say 'yes' to life, and you will be amazed at how life will work for you and not against you.

If you stopped for a moment and gave it a thought, NOW is all you have got in life. You can effortlessly manifest what you want by choosing to accept how life is and how it works. The past is the past. You have no control over it. The same case applies to the future. We often waste time and energy living in the past and worrying too much about the uncertain future. This should change. Acknowledge that life will only work for you when you accept what you can't change and take action on what you can change.

The law of attraction also delves around living in the now and enjoying every moment of it. Most people go through life saying that they will be happy when certain things happen. We often find ourselves saying, "I will be happy when I get money," or "I will be happy when I find my soulmate." The problem with this attitude is that you never stop to enjoy the present moment. You're focused on the future while doing your best to resist the reality of NOW. At the end of the day, you deprive yourself of true happiness and bliss found in enjoying what life has offered you.

Of course, it's good to anticipate good things in your life. However, we should not expect too much to the point where we are dissatisfied with our current lives. So, as you shift your thoughts to think positively and visualize an amazing future, always ensure that you stay in the present moment.

A Word About Desire

We are all creatures of desire. Most of our lives are bound by the desires we have. We desire better lives, happy relationships, more money, joy, and so on. From a spiritual perspective, finding peace is also a desire we often aspire. While we have little control over our wishes, the biggest problem we create for ourselves is attaching ourselves to these desires.

There are different ways of living in the NOW. You might choose to live in joy or misery. Living in misery puts your life on hold and prevents you from manifesting what you want into your life. Conversely, living in joy allows you to enjoy the flow of life and the blessings that come with it.

To attract what you want into your life, you should realize that we consciously and unconsciously send out our desires to the universe.

Similarly, we should strive to fully engage in the present moment. To put the law of attraction and the power of now together, it's vital that you excitedly anticipate a great future while doing your best to love how you're currently living.

War on Fear

When you think about the life you would want to live, fear quickly creeps in and stops you from believing that you can ever enjoy life. Say you're thinking of manifesting more money into your life. Fear will drive you to think of your current financial situation. Perhaps there is a lot you need to handle before you can think of financial freedom. You may also think of the boring career you have and how challenging it is to earn and save money. These are frightening thoughts. Fear prevents us from taking action on our goals.

However, fear is part of life. In some cases, fear is good as it prevents us from doing things that would have caused us pain. For instance, if you weren't afraid of fire, you may risk putting your hand in a fire. But fear is not the main reason why you can't put your hand in a fire. Instead, it's because you're aware that you can get burned. Intelligence and common sense ensure that you don't need to fear to stay away from unnecessary danger.

The fears we often face come in different forms: worry, unease, dread, tension, anxiety, nervousness, and so on. This type of fear is different because it's based on something that might happen. Therefore, while you're doing your best to stay in the present moment, the mind is busy wandering in the future. If you identify yourself with your mind, it means that you will continuously live in fear. Ego will run your life.

Naturally, your ego is always insecure and vulnerable. It perceives itself as constantly in danger. The mind responds through emotions, and the message the body receives from your ego is the false state of mind. You may feel like you're under threat because of the false state of mind. The body responds by generating unnecessary fear.

Acceptance is one effective way of dealing with your fears. What this means is that you should not try to avoid fearful thoughts. Life is full of challenges, and there is nothing you can do about it. Instead of escaping your fears, welcome them and find a way of dealing with them. What you resist will persist. Relax into the present moment by using meditation and breathing exercises. This will liberate you from the false state of the mind that might prevent you from being happy.

Another effective way of dealing with your fears is by learning to appreciate life as it is and expressing gratitude. By expressing gratitude, you allow yourself to focus more on the gifts the universe has bestowed into your life. You will want to focus more on the good side of life. Make a list of the things you're grateful for. This is an exercise you should do every day. A habit of expressing gratitude will also help you see the good even in bad situations. With the positive mindset that you would have developed, you will focus more on learning from the difficult times you face in life. After all, you can't go through life without experiencing challenges. So, it's best that you learn from them and work toward becoming the best version of yourself.

To manifest what you want into your life, strive to change your narrative. Stop focusing on the things you don't want. Sure, fear will drive you to think of the worst that might happen. But when you disassociate yourself from your mind, you will realize that the mind is only creating a false state to prevent you from doing something. Accordingly, you will live in the NOW and focus more on what you really want.

More importantly, retrain your brain to think in the direction that you're heading. The mind has a mind of its own. If you can't control your mind, it will use you. Try not to quickly label situations or people as either right or wrong, good or bad. We all live separate lives with different destinies. The lessons you learn in life might differ from what others learn. And, that's okay. Give people the permission to live their lives without bringing yourself unnecessary pain.

Changing your habits is a process. You can't become the person you want to be overnight. Think of yourself as a work in progress. This means taking the time to improve your life every day. You will be going through a major transition if only you focus on doing the things that bring you an inch closer to your dreams and goals. You should understand that it's okay to be uncomfortable. Things might not work out immediately for you but focus on appreciating your life as it is. Remember, it's a topsy-turvy journey, and there is nothing you can do about it but to adjust and live intentionally. So, get comfortable being uncomfortable.

Chapter 3: Moving Into Alignment and Staying There

When you have identified what you need in life, you need to be in alignment with what you want. Again, this is closely related to what the law of attraction articulates. It's crucial that you are an energetic match with what you want to manifest into your life. This form of alignment requires that you feel good about having or getting whatever it is you wanted. So, instead of being worried or stressed, you should be happy and relaxed with a strong conviction that you will get what you want. This chapter will help you understand how you can move into alignment and stay there without getting distracted.

The idea of aligning yourself with desires implies that you free yourself from the excessive need around that which you strongly desire. It means that you're open to your desires manifesting in varying ways. Moreover, it also means that you're not burdened by how things have to happen. This is because you can't control how things should manifest in your life. Rather, you should be prepared for anything that comes your way and welcome it wholeheartedly.

Theoretically, aligning yourself might sound easy, but in practice, it's not that straightforward. Your natural resistance to change might show up and prevent you from truly believing that everything will fall into place.

It's also worth noting that there are good moments when you feel like things are finally working out. In most cases, these moments don't last for long. We often have those times when we feel motivated to do something. And it is during these times that we feel driven toward our goals. However, this motivation quickly fades away when we face challenges. It's life, right? We tend to live reactively, allowing our beliefs and moods to be affected by the experiences we go through.

Life is not all about achieving a perfect state to manifest what we want. However, it's vital that we focus on uplifting our spirits rather than feeling bad most of the time. In other words, we need to be in alignment instead of being out of it.

Building the right momentum toward aligning yourself in the right way shouldn't be difficult. Your best approach should be to simplify the whole process. This means raising your awareness of your beliefs, thoughts, and feelings that will ensure you attract what you want and weaken the energies that might stop you from reaching your goals.

Determining Your Reasons 'Why'

Attracting what you want in life revolves around 'what' you want. What do you want to manifest now that you're reading this book? Is it love, money, happiness, wealth, abundance? Of course, we all have different desires. Which means your desires will differ from someone else's. The most important thing is to understand that we all have unique paths. So, determining what you really want is a personal approach to knowing what brings you happiness and zeal into your life.

Determining 'what' you want will be the first step that subsequently makes you focus on the 'how.' Before you think about 'how' you will get money, the first step is to determine whether it's money you truly want in your life.

Trusting that everything will work out sounds awesome, and there is no doubt that we all yearn to do the necessary to manifest what we want. However, the mind stops us from fully trusting and believing that we will get what we want. This is one of the main stumbling blocks that deter us from building the momentum we need to manifest. Additionally, another element that might also mess with our quest is our unhealthy attachment with the 'what.' Most people are overly attached to the idea of getting money simply because they think that money will make them happy or that it will change their lives completely. At the end of the day, when this fails to happen, they give up and develop negative attitudes toward money and the overall idea of working hard toward it.

Unconsciously, we normally turn the 'what' into 'how.' We tend to think that whatever we want has to happen so that we can manifest what we want. The reality is that sometimes that which we want might not represent what we truly want. And that's okay. Whatever you're thinking of manifesting is just a fraction of how life can be amazing.

You need to take a step back and understand the reasons behind that which you want. The more you cognize, the deeper reasons why it is easier for you to detach yourself from your desires. More importantly, this also makes it easy for you to align yourself with the energies tied to the desired outcomes NOW. And the best thing is that it doesn't matter what your current situation looks like. It's possible to feel good in the present moment knowing that you've already achieved what you want.

So, why do you want to manifest the desires you have in mind? This is not a simple, Yes or No question. To garner a deeper understanding of why you want something, you need to dig deeper and connect with your emotions. For instance, maybe you want to find love because you're ready to settle down and have a family. Or you want more money to ensure you're happy and less stressed meeting your financial obligations. Think about the reasons behind your quest. Why is it important to you to manifest these things? What makes you think that getting that thing will bring fulfillment into your life? You need to keep asking yourself these questions until you can't go deeper. At this point, you would have reached the core reasons why you need to manifest certain things into your life.

Remember, when determining your reasons why as it's vital that you dwell on the positive. Focus less on what you don't want. The law of attraction requires that you pay attention to what you want and not what you don't want. So, keep your eyes on the prize.

The essence of knowing your 'whys' ensures that you go beyond the feeling tied to what you want. It also helps in bringing clarity into your desires. When you're clear and honest with yourself about what you really want, you will go with the flow of life. Life becomes simple. You will want to live intentionally and purposefully because you know what you want and how to get there. Everything else becomes nothing but a distraction, and you will want to get rid of all these stumbling blocks in your way.

The Universe Will Always Deliver

Let's be honest for a moment here; there is no doubt that we rarely believe that we can actually get what we want. You've been through different relationships, and you can't stop to believe that you can settle down and have a wonderful family. Maybe you're bankrupt, and the last thing you can think about is your life changing and amassing wealth. Admittedly, it sounds like a different world where we are not meant to reside. It's like a fantasy, and our dreams are nothing but mere dreams that will never come true.

Arguably, we all have certain beliefs that we find it daunting to shift or deviate from them. At times, we are too attached to the outcomes of what we want, and we can't think of anything else that might make us happier. We also judge our lives based on our circumstances and our emotional state. The past is also something that we use to gauge whether things will be okay. When things are not turning out as expected, we justify why this might be happening. Interestingly, we have all the reasons to console ourselves that we're just not lucky enough.

With everything going on inside our minds, we are certain that we shouldn't be thinking negatively about ourselves. But we can't help it because it's just how things are unfolding themselves. The problem is that there is so much negative energy around our lives, and we can't see past the challenges we might be facing. Unfortunately, our negative attitudes don't align us with what we want. Instead, we stray away from this alignment, and things get worse. We worry too much that our dreams will never come true. We also worry that we've messed up everything and that life will not change as we desire.

The beauty of life is that you don't have to master taking control of your emotions or eliminating self-limiting beliefs completely for you to attract what you want. You don't have to perfect your life. Negative emotions surrounding your life will always be there. The same case applies to the self-limiting beliefs that hold you back. It's the nature of life, and there is a lot we need to do to continuously think positively and attract what we want.

You can change your narrative by just being receptive to the universe, even if you don't know how it will happen. Even believing for a few minutes that it's possible can make a huge difference. The more you enter that space where you trust, believe, and receive what you want, the more likely you will manifest your desires. You need to trust that everything will be okay without worrying about what you have no control over. Amazing things will happen in your life because the universe always delivers. All you need to do is to believe that it's possible.

Strengthen your faith and appreciate the fact that there are things happening behind the scenes to streamline your life. Sure, you don't know what is happening, but deep inside, you trust that something good will show up. You don't need to understand the 'how'; the 'how' will take care of itself.

In those beautiful moments of believing and trusting that the universe will deliver, positive energy of manifestation will fill your space. You will start living in the NOW with less worry about the future. You will also be more receptive to the things happening in your life. When you get to this point, the power of manifestation will transform your life forever.

Dealing With Conflicting Energies

Over time, good things will start happening in your life. Your relationships may get better, and you may start seeing the light at the end of the tunnel in your finances. These are great signs that you're on the right path. Trust builds, and your belief system will start to shift. You will also have a positive attitude toward everything going on.

However, you should realize that it won't be a smooth sail all the way. Energies that were once holding you back will keep resurfacing. And the worst thing is that, at times, you won't notice their effects on your mission.

Somewhere along the way, you may find yourself worrying that you did something wrong. You could feel like you've messed up and erased all the progress you've made. Negativity will build-up, and if you fail to take action, you might fall back to where you started. When this happens, it's crucial to remind yourself that there is nothing wrong going on. Challenges are part of the process, so it's best that you learn how to welcome them. We all have our low moments in life, even when everything is going smoothly. The best thing we can do to lift our spirits is to understand that life will never be smooth. There are ups and downs that we have to face, and it's during our weak moments that we leverage our strengths to see past difficulties.

In those trying moments, strive to understand what the experience might be teaching you. Don't avoid negative feelings. Connect with them and find out what life might be teaching you. Go with the flow. Eventually, you will realize that there is some energy worked to change your life in one way or another. After all, what doesn't kill you will make you stronger.

Generally, life would have been more exciting if you could just believe in something, and it manifests right away. Well, sometimes it's this easy, but on rare occasions. Most of the time, we have to deal with the resistance that comes from within. You want something, but your mind thinks the other way. Worse, it might give you all sorts of reasons not to believe that you can manifest what you want into your life. But there is hope as things get better with time. With time, you will find it easier to move into a space where you believe and trust that the universe will deliver. When unfortunate events occur, you won't be surprised or overwhelmed. You will be more accepting of these circumstances, and that you will strive to shift your attention to what you want.

Aligning yourself with your manifestations won't be easy at first. Your human, and all along, you've shaped your beliefs and attitudes based on your past. It will take some time to change this. Be patient as you go through this transition. Remember to celebrate the manifestations that give you a reason to believe that you're on the right path. The little positive energy that radiates within you can snowball gradually.

Chapter 4: Get Out of Your Own Way - Overcome Self-Sabotage

To most people, self-sabotage is a defense mechanism. When good things fail to manifest in your life, you have all the excuses you need to change direction and walk a different path. Often, we allow our brains to control us. Unconsciously, we find ourselves holding on to failure, loss, rejection, and fear. This prevents us from staying motivated toward the big goals that we have set for ourselves. Perhaps you thought of starting a business or changing careers. The thought that you might fail in the process can quickly derail your progress.

Fortunately, you can get out of your own way and overcome self-sabotage behaviors. The worst thing about self-sabotage is that it creates unnecessary pain in our lives. Fear, failure, doubt, rejection, and so on can make you feel like you're not living your best life. At some point, you may start doubting yourself, wondering whether there is something that you're not doing to succeed.

Self-sabotage behavior can take different forms. For some, it can take the form of avoidance or procrastination. For others, it might look like relieving stress in unhealthy ways, like wasting money, overeating, or abusing alcohol or drugs. To manifest what you want in your life, it's vital that you learn how to overcome such behaviors.

Why Do We Self-Sabotage Our Efforts?

It's a common thing to find people feeling anxious and stressed when trying to accomplish certain goals. When the worst happens, they get angry with themselves and feel discouraged in the process. The negative feelings they experience prevent them from doing what they need to do to thrive. Basically, these are signs of self-sabotage.

The moment you doubt yourself, your self-esteem and self-confidence is eroded. Now, with every subsequent failure you experience in trying to accomplish your goal, you affirm to yourself that indeed you're a failure or that you can't achieve something. In other words, destructive behavior undermines your efforts. You may not notice it at first, but when such behaviors become a habit, they develop into psychological self-harm.

We tend to self-sabotage because of our low self-esteem. The cause can vary from one person to another, but the effects are similar: Believing that you're not worthy of success, joy, and happiness, or feelings of worthlessness, and even escalating to self-hatred.

You may be troubled that your failure might mean that your friends and family will think less of you. You may also think that your success might make your colleagues jealous of you. These negative feelings and thoughts often lead to negative self-talk. This further fuels the fears and beliefs you've developed over time.

Most individuals self-sabotage as a way of taking control of the situation they might be facing. It gives them a reason to think that they are taking control of the situation. For instance, by procrastinating things, you give yourself a short-term boost in your confidence that you can accomplish something. But ultimately, such behaviors are destructive.

In line with the notion of manifesting what you want in life, self-sabotage can hold you back. You may have set goals and decided to commit yourself to a particular mission. Unconsciously, your mind might stop you from taking action on what you think is important. For instance, if you're trying to manifest love, self-sabotage will make you ignore potential partners. If you're thinking of finding yourself a new job, self-sabotage will drive you to procrastinate the need to fine-tune your resume.

Of course, it's natural to get disheartened or frustrated when you fail to manifest what you want. But it's important to remember that you're not alone. This happens to everyone. The best thing you can do is maintain a positive attitude toward what you really want. If you're not manifesting what you want, patience and hard work will take you all the way. The universe will never fail you.

Overcoming Self-Defeating Behavior

To stop self-sabotaging yourself, you need to shift your mindset. Instead of allowing negative thoughts to fill your mind, you should consider shifting your thoughts. It is through a positive mindset that you are better placed to manifest what you truly want. The following pointers should help you get started.

Uncover Self-Destructive Behavior

Start by digging the reasons behind your self-sabotaging behavior. What is that thing that is holding you back? What's stopping you from believing that you can accomplish your goals? Your reasons are tied to the desires you have in mind. For example, if you're looking to manifest abundance, self-sabotage will drive you to think of all the reasons why this can't happen for you. Strive to understand what the other side of you believes. Why does your mind trick you into believing that you can't attract abundance your way?

Determine the reasons behind your destructive behaviors. Make a list of these things. In terms of abundance, for example, your subconscious mind might think that there is a lot you lack for you to live a fulfilled life. Maybe you're not happy in your relationship or that your businesses are not paying off. Perhaps you've developed a habit of abusing alcohol.

Armed with a list of the reasons why you might not be doing something, challenge yourself to go against your subconscious mind. Do something you initially told yourself you couldn't manage. Face your fears and take control of your mind.

Recognize Self-Sabotaging Habits

Now, once you've identified some of the destructive behaviors holding you back, the next step is to develop new productive habits. It takes time to develop a habit. So, you need to be patient to make changes in your life that will stick. Some common destructive habits that you will have to work on include procrastination, perfectionism, and negative self-talk.

Make Significant Changes to Your Life

In addition to replacing old habits with new healthier ones, you should consider making more significant changes. Particularly, find a way of reframing your mindset. Do your best to develop a positive attitude every day. Affirmations can help you start the day on a positive note. Raise your awareness of your self-talk and aim to make this positive. Every time you catch yourself thinking negatively about yourself, reaffirm to yourself that you can become better. You're a work in progress; keep focusing on improving yourself one day at a time.

Creating a vision board is also a great way of developing a positive mindset around the things you wish to manifest. With this vision board, you can paint how you would want your future to look. Through the power of visualization, you can start shifting your mindset to start believing that it's possible to attract what you want. Ensure you notice the small achievements you make along the way as they draw the right energies that bring you in alignment with your manifestations.

Take Time to Self-Reflect

Knowing that you're making progress in life is fulfilling. Consequently, while taking time to change your destructive behaviors, you need to find time to self-reflect. Monitor whether you're developing productive habits that guarantee you don't just live but also thrive. Similarly, notice when certain behaviors stop you from thinking positively and find out why. An ideal way of monitoring your progress is by journaling regularly. Write down your experiences, and you will find it easy to know what works and what doesn't. This way, you can make the necessary changes to improve.

Connect With Your Inner Positive Voice

An integral part of dealing with self-sabotage requires that you silence your inner critic. This is the small voice inside you that continuously reminds you that you can't achieve something. You can be great. In fact, you were born to be great. Therefore, it's important not to allow your inner critic to get the best of you. Stop the negative self-talk inside you and replace this voice with a more rewarding, positive self-talk. You can do this with the help of meditation. Thought-stopping exercises will give you power over your thoughts. As a result, you will learn how to silence the inner chatter in your mind and find the peace you need. The mind can also be exercised like any other muscle. The more you exercise it, the stronger it gets. So, focus on training your brain to think positively.

Chapter 5: The Secret Behind Manifesting

It might take some time to manifest what you want in life. When this happens, it's normal to find yourself wondering whether there is something you should be doing to notice positive changes in your path. If you're not careful, you might even choose to give up altogether, thinking that the power of manifesting doesn't work for you. But you should understand that you're not going through such a dilemma on your own. There are thousands of other people struggling to make the power of manifesting work for them. In fact, most people have tried to apply the law of attraction, but they haven't been successful. Indeed, it's disappointing when you've been spending all your precious time visualizing your ideal life, but nothing works.

So, here we unveil for you the secret that you should apply to make manifesting work for you.

Ask, Believe, Receive

The secret behind manifesting what you want in life is based on the phrase, 'ask, believe, receive.' Chances are that you've decided to read this book because your manifestations are not materializing. This means that you're still searching for that one secret that will change your life forever.

As you look to understand how to apply this secret, it's important to understand that it's not your fault you're not manifesting anything in your life. It could be that you've been misinformed all along about how to manifest your dream life.

When you think of the phrase, 'ask, believe, receive,' it sounds simple. But it's not as straightforward as you might be thinking. The first step is asking. Of course, this might be the easiest thing to do. We all have an idea of what we want in life. So, making your requests to the universe shouldn't be that of a problem. The last step is receiving. Again, this is also not a difficult thing to do because you simply need to welcome positive changes into your life.

Now, the biggest challenge we face is the believing part. This is where most people trip. Believing is not easy because you need to have faith in the unseen for you to manifest what you want. Say you want to manifest wealth. Since you haven't manifested it and you haven't seen it, it becomes daunting to even think that it's possible.

To most people, they believe in the idea that seeing is believing. This means that you will only believe in something when you finally see it with your own eyes. But this contradicts the whole idea of attracting the life you want. For you to receive (and see), you must take a bold step and believe.

Believing in the Unseen

So, how do you start believing in the unseen? Rather than lazing around expecting money to fall in your laps, it's easier for you to find proof that the strategy you're applying works. Think of it this way; you've learned to believe that your trustworthy friend will come through and help you when you need them most. Often, you can't think of the worst because there is some certainty that they will help out. In the same way, you can start believing that the law of attraction will be there to save you when you need help. It doesn't matter what you desire. By making this law your best friend, you bring clarity and certainty into your life. To you, nothing will seem impossible.

It's vital to open your eyes to the cues from the universe that the law of attraction works. Notice the small positive changes in your life and acknowledge them. The more you see and connect with evidence that the law works, the more you strengthen your belief system. Over time, you will learn to trust the universe to deliver.

Take Action

Identify your heart's desires and focus your energies there. While doing this, strive to be deliberate with your actions. You don't have to postpone your happiness into a space that is nonexistent in the present moment. Quit saying that you will be happy and content when this and that happens. Live in the NOW. Act as if you have what you desire. Live like you already have what you want to manifest. If it's money you're looking to manifest, start acting like you're rich. Stop living like you lack something. Live abundantly, and you will align yourself with the right energies to attract what you want.

Be Autonomous

The beauty of manifestation is that everything is yours to decide. This means that you should leverage the power of choice to create the life you desire. Identify what you want in life and decide to live intentionally. This demands that you find clarity in what you want and going for it by taking action. The most important thing to remember is that you should be bold when asking the universe. This means you shouldn't settle for anything less. A strong belief system is what you need to see with conviction that you already have that which you strongly desire.

Chapter 6: Live Life Fully

It's never too late to start living again. Perhaps you're thinking that there is a lot that you need to do for you to start enjoying life once again. But the truth is that you were born to live an adventure. Maybe life has not been easy for you, and you've been stressing over it. Guess what? That's life. You were born to counter these challenges, the hardships, and the pains that come with them. At the end of it all, it is the joy of accomplishing something and overcoming the adversities.

Most people coast through life feeling empty and depressed. If you look around you, you will notice there are people who are just there to pass the time. To put it more specifically, they show no signs of living. Rarely will you find these people showing some excitement about how life is and the new day they are gifted. Interestingly, they cling to memories of what life used to mean to them. But deep down, they long to live life once again. It's sad!

The first step to living your life more fully is accepting one scary fact: You become alive again by welcoming pain. Life is a struggle. That's a fact. So, to experience life, you must understand that pain is integral to keep you alive. You experience joy when you overcome the hardships of life. You build your muscles when you stretch beyond the normal limits. Courage is also built in the face of danger. So, you must get comfortable being uncomfortable.

When you choose to live a comfortable life, you will get bored sooner or later. Why? Because there is nothing challenging about it. There is no reason to enjoy the thrill of accomplishing something that you've been working hard to bring into your life. Therefore, give up the idea of living a comfortable life. Life is all about pressing on. You may not have achieved your dreams, but keep pressing on. Expect the best to happen by trusting your good friend, the law of attraction. The universe will not disappoint you.

Take a look at the most successful people you often admire; these people stand out because they take risks and embrace failure in everything they do. They learn from their failures, and they choose never to get comfortable. Well, now that you know the secret path to this life, you can also live the life of your dreams, if you want.

To this point, you know what you want in life. But the question is, are you ready to pay the price. Living your life more fully comes with a hefty price tag. It's easy to assume that you will change your life by following a specific strategy or that you will live a happy and content life. However, the most challenging decision you need to make is to decide to live. This means accepting the fact that pain will make you grow. The point here is that manifesting all that you need in life comes at a cost. You must be prepared to pay the price and live your best life. And you've heard it more often than not - No pain? No gain! Right? It's a well-known fact. So, apply it in your life and live again.

Final Thoughts

Given the opportunity, there is no doubt that we would strive to live our best lives. We all want to achieve our dreams and find purpose in the life we live. But this never comes that easily. We often have to overcome challenges in our life path to get to where we want. In fact, we've been brought up with different notions surrounding our deepest desires. "Life is not easy," "money doesn't grow on trees," "hard work pays," and so on. With these perceptions, we go through life knowing that everything is all about overcoming challenges. Perhaps this negative mindset that we're brought up with alters how we view life and how we can manifest what we want.

The problem with the negative mindset that we've developed over time is that it drives us to reinforce the fears we have around our innermost desires. You want to manifest money, but it's easy to assume that money doesn't bring you happiness or that money doesn't come easily. So, you end up consoling yourself and finding proof of your negative perceptions about money. The worst thing that happens is that the universe listens to you through the vibrations you radiate.

The negative energy you radiate prevents you from staying aligned with what you want. Instead of focusing on what you want, you're focusing on what you don't want. The universe listens, and it vibrates through your energy frequencies. You're afraid of failing, and guess what happens? You fail in what you're doing. When you're afraid that you might never achieve your goals, the worst happens, and your goals seem far-fetched. That's how the universe works. Like attracts like, and you will always attract what you want into your life.

If you want to attract joy, bliss, abundance, money, fame, wealth, and love, etc., you need to focus on what you want. In other words, align yourself with what you really want to manifest into your life. Quit thinking of the worst that might happen. Change your narrative and start visualizing your best life. See yourself living your best life in the present moment.

This brings us to the importance of making the best out of the present moment you have in your life. You only have NOW to enjoy life and make things happen. The past is the past. Forget about what happened because you have no control over it. Similarly, the same case applies to your future. Stop worrying about the 'what ifs.' You can't exist in the future or the past and expect to enjoy life. Use meditation techniques to bring your mind to the present moment.

Learn to express gratitude for the things you have in your life. Before you start manifesting what you want, express gratitude. Be thankful that you're alive. Vibrate with positive energies about your life, and you will see your life transform. What you give is what you get. So, choose to radiate positive energies, and in turn, the universe will bring what you want into your life.

You now have all the tools you need to start manifesting what you want into your life. The first step is to ask the universe what you want. Be clear about it. You can't just say you want to make a lot of money. Be specific about it, and if possible, paint it on your vision board. Write it down how much you want. Asking is not as challenging as the second step of believing. Here, you need to believe with conviction that what you want will indeed manifest no matter how long it takes.

Perhaps, you may be worried because there is a lot going on in your life, and it's not easy for you to believe that you can attract what you want. You do not need to worry about how things will work out. The only thing you need to do is to BELIEVE. The same way you trust a true friend to always be there for you is the same belief you should have when trusting the universe to come through for you. Use the law of attraction. Practice it every day and make it a part of your life. The most successful people have proven it to work, so be sure that it will also work for you if you apply it the right way.

As you transition and align yourself with what you want to manifest, you need to remember that there will be conflicting energies to overcome. Yes, you want to attract something good into your life, but the mind will think otherwise. Your self-sabotaging behavior will affirm to you that you can't live the life of your dreams. The mind has

Final Thoughts

Given the opportunity, there is no doubt that we would strive to live our best lives. We all want to achieve our dreams and find purpose in the life we live. But this never comes that easily. We often have to overcome challenges in our life path to get to where we want. In fact, we've been brought up with different notions surrounding our deepest desires. "Life is not easy," "money doesn't grow on trees," "hard work pays," and so on. With these perceptions, we go through life knowing that everything is all about overcoming challenges. Perhaps this negative mindset that we're brought up with alters how we view life and how we can manifest what we want.

The problem with the negative mindset that we've developed over time is that it drives us to reinforce the fears we have around our innermost desires. You want to manifest money, but it's easy to assume that money doesn't bring you happiness or that money doesn't come easily. So, you end up consoling yourself and finding proof of your negative perceptions about money. The worst thing that happens is that the universe listens to you through the vibrations you radiate.

The negative energy you radiate prevents you from staying aligned with what you want. Instead of focusing on what you want, you're focusing on what you don't want. The universe listens, and it vibrates through your energy frequencies. You're afraid of failing, and guess what happens? You fail in what you're doing. When you're afraid that you might never achieve your goals, the worst happens, and your goals seem far-fetched. That's how the universe works. Like attracts like, and you will always attract what you want into your life.

If you want to attract joy, bliss, abundance, money, fame, wealth, and love, etc., you need to focus on what you want. In other words, align yourself with what you really want to manifest into your life. Quit thinking of the worst that might happen. Change your narrative and start visualizing your best life. See yourself living your best life in the present moment.

75

This brings us to the importance of making the best out of the present moment you have in your life. You only have NOW to enjoy life and make things happen. The past is the past. Forget about what happened because you have no control over it. Similarly, the same case applies to your future. Stop worrying about the 'what ifs.' You can't exist in the future or the past and expect to enjoy life. Use meditation techniques to bring your mind to the present moment.

Learn to express gratitude for the things you have in your life. Before you start manifesting what you want, express gratitude. Be thankful that you're alive. Vibrate with positive energies about your life, and you will see your life transform. What you give is what you get. So, choose to radiate positive energies, and in turn, the universe will bring what you want into your life.

You now have all the tools you need to start manifesting what you want into your life. The first step is to ask the universe what you want. Be clear about it. You can't just say you want to make a lot of money. Be specific about it, and if possible, paint it on your vision board. Write it down how much you want. Asking is not as challenging as the second step of believing. Here, you need to believe with conviction that what you want will indeed manifest no matter how long it takes.

Perhaps, you may be worried because there is a lot going on in your life, and it's not easy for you to believe that you can attract what you want. You do not need to worry about how things will work out. The only thing you need to do is to BELIEVE. The same way you trust a true friend to always be there for you is the same belief you should have when trusting the universe to come through for you. Use the law of attraction. Practice it every day and make it a part of your life. The most successful people have proven it to work, so be sure that it will also work for you if you apply it the right way.

As you transition and align yourself with what you want to manifest, you need to remember that there will be conflicting energies to overcome. Yes, you want to attract something good into your life, but the mind will think otherwise. Your self-sabotaging behavior will affirm to you that you can't live the life of your dreams. The mind has a mind of its own, and it will drive you to think negatively even when you want to attract the best into your life. Accordingly, it's imperative that you learn how to silence your inner critic and live in the space where you believe in abundance, happiness, love, and the power of manifesting all that you want in life.

Are you ready to light up and live again? If your answer is yes, then you need to be prepared to pay the price. Living life fully demands that you get comfortable being uncomfortable. Pain is part of life, and you need to learn to live with it. Learn from your failures and do your best to grow through pain. Arguably, it is through difficulties that we become the best version of ourselves. You were born to live. So, do your best to manifest all that you want. Your current circumstances shouldn't stop you from moving forward. Just move into alignment and stay there.

Good luck!

If you enjoyed this book in anyway, an honest

References

Bible Hub. (2021). *Matthew 7:7 ask, and it will be given to you; seek, and you will find; knock, and the door will be opened to you.* Bible Hub: Search, Read, Study the Bible in Many Languages. https://biblehub.com/matthew/7-7.htm

Literary Devices. (2019, May 25). *A journey of a thousand miles begins with a single step.* https://literarydevices.net/a-journey-of-a-thousand-miles-begins-with-a-single-step/

www.ingramcontent.com/pod-product-compliance
Lightning Source LLC
Chambersburg PA
CBHW030915080526
44589CB00010B/318